MW00464109

MONEY CHANGES

BY ANDREW GUNN

INTRODUCTION

Imagine being able to walk into a supermarket, fill a cart with whatever groceries you want, and simply push the loaded cart out the door. You don't pass through a checkout, nor do you hand over cash, a credit card, or anything else. And yet the supermarket owner gives you a cheery wave as you head for the parking lot with your supplies. You have just paid for those groceries without having to do a thing.

If this were possible (and it is), would you want to shop this way? Would it affect what you decided to buy or when you bought it? What might be some advantages and disadvantages of shopping like this?

The way we pay for things has changed many times over the years. The kinds of things people buy continually changes too. Someone living a hundred years ago would never have been able to purchase ordinary household goods from another continent. Yet today millions of people use the Internet to purchase items from anywhere in the world.

Before money as we know it existed, people traded in **commodities**. Roman soldiers, for example, were paid with bars of salt. In fact, the word *salary* comes from the Latin word for salt.

Each method of payment has advantages and disadvantages. The way we think about these benefits and drawbacks helps us decide which kind of money to use. We may use different forms of money for different kinds of purchases. This includes a form of payment that we are very familiar with: cash.

In the future, advances in technology might remove the need for supermarkets to have checkouts.

CHAPTER 1

MONEY BEFORE THE DIGITAL AGE

Before the digital age, the main way to pay for purchases was with paper, including cash and checks. Even early credit cards used paper. However, that doesn't mean there weren't big changes in how people spent their money.

CASH

For hundreds of years, people all over the world have used cash to pay for goods and services. It's not hard to understand why. Banknotes, or paper money, and coins are accepted almost everywhere. Cash can be used to pay for nearly any purchase, whether it is a goat or a go-kart, a harmonica or a haircut. Paying with cash is also fast and reliable: People being paid know immediately that they've received exactly the amount of money they're owed.

Another advantage of cash is that it's easier to keep track of the money you're spending when you can see it. Studies have shown that people tend to spend less when they use cash compared with other forms of money.

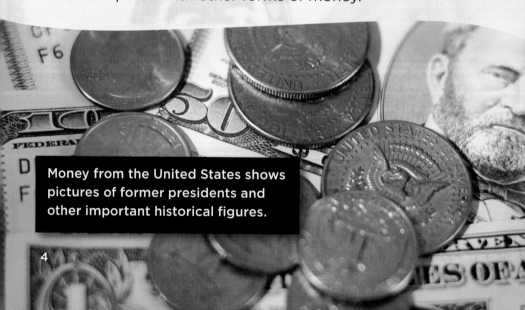

Money from the United States shows pictures of former presidents and other important historical figures.

But cash has **limitations**. Most people keep their money in bank accounts. In the past, people could not access their money if there was no bank nearby or the bank was not open. In 1967, banks began to provide Automated Teller Machines (ATMs) to overcome this problem. ATMs, which can be set up almost anywhere that has a power supply, make cash available 24 hours a day.

However, cash has other disadvantages. For example, it's not ideal to use cash when making expensive purchases. Imagine how tricky it would be to carry around enough cash to pay for a house or a car. It would also be hard to retrieve such a large amount of cash if it were lost or stolen. Cash is not useful for buying items from a distance either. **Vendors** discourage people from sending cash by mail because, again, the cash could easily be lost or stolen.

Factors such as these have led to the development of new forms of payment.

EXTREME ATMS

The first ATMs were set up in large cities. However, today they can be found in all kinds of locations. There's one in Nagchu County, Tibet, more than 14,000 feet above sea level. There's another in Ein Bokek beside the Dead Sea in Israel. That's almost 1,400 feet below sea level. You'll find an ATM in the world's northernmost town, Longyearbyen, in Norway. There's even an ATM at McMurdo Station in Antarctica!

CHECKS

One form of payment that has come into use in recent times is the check. A check is a piece of paper that is **imprinted** with the check writer's name, address, and bank account details. It is basically a written instruction that tells a bank to pay money from the check writer's account into another person's account.

A check can be more convenient than cash because it may be for any value. It can also be safer because it names the person or business that should receive the money. Also, the bank can cancel payment if a check is lost or stolen.

However, checks aren't a perfect solution. The person who receives a check can't be sure that the person who wrote it has enough money in his or her account. The receiver has to wait until the bank clears the check, which may take several days. If there isn't enough money in the account, the check will "bounce," and the person who wrote the check will be charged a fee.

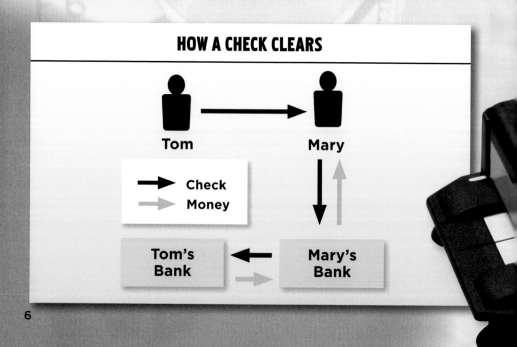

HOW A CHECK CLEARS

Tom → Mary

→ Check
→ Money

Tom's Bank ← Mary's Bank

THE FIRST CREDIT CARDS

Credit cards are another alternative to cash. In the 1920s, department stores began offering customers cards made from cardboard or metal, and by the 1960s, most banks offered plastic credit cards.

People don't use real money when they use credit cards. The credit-card company, often a bank, pays the vendor on the purchaser's behalf. Each credit card has a limit, which is the maximum value the person can spend.

Before electronic banking, vendors took a paper copy of the credit card. The purchaser signed the copy, and the vendor checked that the signature matched the one on the card.

However, people could steal credit cards and **forge** the cardholders' signatures. There was also no guarantee that a purchaser had enough credit to make the payment. The purchaser, the vendor, and the credit-card company needed to be connected electronically.

In the past, vendors used a device called an imprinter to copy details from purchasers' credit cards.

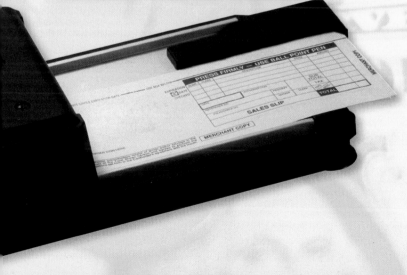

CHAPTER 2

ELECTRONIC MONEY

In the digital age, many people have moved on from paper money. Instead of cash and checks, we use plastic, such as credit and debit cards. But the difference is much more significant than a simple change of material.

CREDIT AND DEBIT CARDS

Modern credit cards work differently from the early versions. The vendor does not take a copy of the card, but instead swipes the card through a device that is electronically connected to the credit-card company's computer. The credit-card company can instantly **decline** the **transaction** if the card number is **invalid**, the card has expired, or the purchaser has exceeded his or her credit limit.

Purchasers either sign their names or enter their secret personal identification numbers (PINs) to complete transactions. This makes the process more **secure**.

However, there is still a security risk if someone else finds out the cardholder's PIN. This is not the only drawback to using a credit card.

(b) Exactostock/SuperStock

Credit and debit cards store important data about the cardholder's account on a magnetic stripe on the back of the card.

Credit-card companies charge interest on the money they lend. This is a percentage of the amount spent. Each month, cardholders receive bills listing their **expenditures**. They must pay at least part of their balances. As the balances increase, the amounts of interest they are charged increase as well.

When people borrow money, they are in debt, and if they **accumulate** too much debt, they can become bankrupt. This means that they owe so much money that they are unable to pay it back. This is a serious risk for credit-card users.

The electronic debit card is the cousin of the credit card. The transaction works the same way, but instead of borrowing the money from a credit-card company, the money is taken directly out of the purchaser's bank account. This makes it harder for people to spend more than their salaries allow.

Unfortunately, debit cards don't entirely prevent overspending as people still tend to buy more when they can't see the money they're spending. So what happens when people can spend money without even leaving home?

SHOPPING ONLINE

Turkish carpets, musical instruments, shoes from other countries—all types of manufactured goods are available for purchase through computers thanks to the Internet and electronic money.

The **consumer** enters his or her credit or debit card details into a purchasing page on an online company's Web site. Overseas goods may not need to be paid for in foreign **currency** because some Web sites have a simple mathematical formula that converts the price to the purchaser's currency.

Shopping online makes spending money even easier. Some people might spend more online from the comfort of their own homes than they do when shopping with credit or debit cards in stores.

However, some things aren't practical to buy from a distance. It's hard to make sure that those new shoes fit when they're on the other side of the world!

The most popular online purchases include books, clothes, and DVDs.

Sometimes shopping online can be more expensive than shopping in a store. Online purchases often have shipping fees added to them, which can be very high if the product comes from far away or needs to be delivered quickly.

Security, particularly identity theft, is a more serious issue for online shoppers. Thieves can steal other people's credit card or bank account details over the computer. They use that information to buy things or even to apply for more credit cards. Proving identity theft and reversing the charges can be a difficult and lengthy process. As online shopping becomes more common, thieves are coming up with new ways to access people's private information.

Shopping over the Internet is popular despite the security issues. Its speed, variety of goods, and convenience make spending money fast and easy. Believe it or not, though, new methods of payment are even faster.

INTERNET SPENDING, 2006-2011

Online retail sales (billions)

- $300
- $200
- $100

- 2006 — $149
- 2007 — $179
- 2008 — $210
- 2009 — $216
- 2010 — $251
- 2011 — $287

Years

When Internet shopping first started, people were very cautious, but now more and more people are using online shopping to purchase all kinds of things.

CHAPTER 3

MONEY IN THE FUTURE

It is very easy to spend money these days. We can use a credit card and press a few buttons. Soon, however, we may not have to do even that.

SMART CARDS

The contactless smart card is faster and easier to use than the credit or debit card. It does not need to be swiped, nor does it require a signature or a PIN. It only needs to be near a smart-card reader.

The smart card has a microchip that stores information, such as the cardholder's account balance. When people use smart cards to make payments, the money is taken directly from their accounts. This type of payment is already used in some areas, such as public transportation. People simply hold smart cards by readers when they board buses or subways. Smart cards are beginning to be used in other places, such as fast-food outlets and gas stations.

Security can be a problem with smart cards. Anyone could find and use someone else's smart card because it doesn't require a PIN.

RFID

A newer form of contactless smart card uses a technology called Radio Frequency Identification (RFID), which sends radio waves to read information on the card. RFID cards can be read from much farther away than regular smart cards.

This technology is already being used to collect road tolls in many places around the world. Drivers' account information is stored on tags in their vehicles. When a vehicle passes a tollbooth, an RFID reader scans the tag and automatically deducts the toll from the vehicle owner's account. This has helped reduce traffic jams, particularly during rush hours. Many drivers also use RFID tags on keychains to pay for gasoline.

RFID is also used in stores to track inventory, and soon it may be used to make other purchases.

RFID tags on clothes make it easy for this store owner to keep track of inventory.

An RFID tag could be attached to every product in a store. This would make shopping much faster because each item would not need to be scanned individually. An entire shopping cart of products could be scanned instantly.

Shoppers could load their carts with items and simply wheel them out the door. As they passed the RFID reader, it would scan their smart cards and all the tags on the goods. The total cost of the goods would be deducted from their accounts.

While this technology offers unmatched convenience, it also poses serious security risks. Thieves could scan shoppers' cards and steal the money in their accounts. There are also privacy concerns about companies using the data to track customers' spending. Until there are solutions to these problems, RFID use should be limited.

GROCERY SHOPPING WITH RFID

1. The RFID reader sends out radio waves.
2. A grocery item with an RFID tag sends back information on the price to the RFID reader.
3. The reader sends information about how much you've spent to your bank.

Grocery item with RFID tag

RFID reader

Bank

CELL PHONES

Another development is using cell phones to make
payments. Many cell phones already connect to the
Internet. People could use their cell phones to check
whether they had enough money in their accounts. Since
prices often fluctuate, they could then use their phones to
search for the best bargains. After deciding where to shop,
they could quickly and easily pay for the items—all with a
single device!

There are, of course, drawbacks to this form of payment
too. If you lost your phone, someone else could find it and
use it to make purchases. As the owner of the phone, you
would be responsible until you could prove that you did not
buy the items. Security risks are currently greater than with
other forms of payment because the technology is still very
new. Effective **safeguards** have not been put into place yet.

CONCLUSION

People today can choose between many different forms of payment. To make the best decision, they need to consider many different factors, such as speed, convenience, and security. Each person has his or her own set of priorities when it comes to spending money.

One important thing for people to keep in mind is how easily they want to be able to spend their money. Some people have trouble controlling the amount of money they spend, which makes it easy to get into debt. These people may need to limit their spending. Cash can help with this since it's not possible to spend more than you have with you. However, cash can be inconvenient if you need to have exact change, such as for a bus fare. A contactless public transportation card would be much easier.

Every form of payment has advantages and disadvantages. It's easy to charge expenses, such as restaurant meals, to a credit card. However, unless the credit card bill is paid promptly, interest accumulates, adding to the cost. Online shopping often offers a wider choice and more discounts, but it is necessary to consider extra costs such as shipping fees, and you may not be happy with your purchase when it arrives. Shopping online also makes shoppers vulnerable to security risks, such as identity theft. Checks have fewer security risks, but they are not accepted everywhere.

Paying with a smart card or a cell phone also carries risks. If you lose your card or phone, it may be difficult and time-consuming to access your money and get a new device. Whichever form of money we choose, we need to understand its good and bad points. Every decision we make affects how, when, and where we spend money.

Respond to Reading

Summarize

Use important details from *Money Changes* to summarize the factors that influence how people use money. Your graphic organizer may help you.

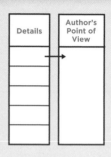

Text Evidence

1. What characteristics tell you that *Money Changes* is an informational article? **GENRE**

2. In *Money Changes*, what is the author's point of view on the alternatives to using cash? What important details in the text show this? **AUTHOR'S POINT OF VIEW**

3. The word *unfortunately* on page 9 includes the root *fortunate*. Use the meaning of the prefix and suffix added to the root word to help you define *unfortunately*. **ROOT WORDS**

4. Write about the arguments the author makes for and against contactless payment systems in Chapter 3. Do the reasons presented convince you to use one of those systems? Use details from the text to support your choice. **WRITE ABOUT READING**

Compare Texts

Read a persuasive article in favor of using cash as currency.

CASH IS HERE TO STAY

I've used a lot of different forms of money, and there's one thing that I'm sure of. Cash will always be with us, no matter how many new methods of payment are invented.

Cash has a long history in the United States. In 1729, Benjamin Franklin, one of the founding fathers, wrote a booklet in favor of paper currency. He believed cash would help people to buy and sell goods and increase trade. However, paper money was outlawed in the colonies under British rule. The United States didn't issue its own paper currency until 1861.

The world has transformed in countless ways over the centuries. We now have electricity, automobiles, airplanes, and computers. All these inventions hugely affect the way we live. But paper money, that is cash, still makes buying and selling all kinds of goods and services easy.

In some situations, it is much easier to pay with cash.

19

Other forms of money have become popular over time. But their popularity never lasts. Checks, for instance, are quickly falling out of use. In fact, they are rarely used in many European countries. In Sweden high fees are charged for using checks. This is to encourage people to use more modern ways of paying. However, you can still walk into a store in Sweden and pay with cash.

It's the same with credit cards. Once, the latest, smartest way to pay was with paper-copy credit card transactions. You don't see many of those anymore, but you do see dollar bills, nickels, dimes, and quarters—cash.

Electronic payments can be very quick and easy, but they are not always practical. A person could pay a babysitter with an electronic transfer, but cash is much more convenient.

It's convenient to have cash on hand to pay for services such as babysitting.

It's true that people use cash less often these days. Studies confirm that cash use declines every year. However, even if it declined by 17 percent every five years, people in the United States would still spend more than dollars 1 billion dollars in cash per year for the next 200 years.

Cash cannot be used in every situation. You can't use it for online shopping, for instance. However, that is a benefit as well as a drawback. It's much harder for people to go into debt when they are paying with cash since they cannot spend more cash than they have.

Many things have changed in the centuries since Franklin explained the appeal of cash. Other forms of payment have come and gone, and new ones will continue to do so. However, none has endured as well as cash.

Make Connections

In *Cash Is Here to Stay,* why does the author believe that some people will always use cash?
ESSENTIAL QUESTION

What do *Money Changes* and *Cash Is Here to Stay* tell you about the factors that influence the forms of money that people choose to use? **TEXT TO TEXT**

Glossary

accumulate *(uh-KYEW-myuh-layt)* increase gradually *(page 9)*

commodities *(kuh-MAH-duh-teez)* goods or services considered valuable *(page 3)*

consumer *(kuhn-SEW-muhr)* someone who uses something *(page 10)*

currency *(KUHR-uhn-see)* a form of payment; money *(page 10)*

decline *(di-KLIGHN)* reject or refuse *(page 8)*

expenditures *(ek-SPEN-di-chuhrz)* amounts that have been spent *(page 9)*

forge *(fawrj)* make a copy of something while knowing that the copy will be used falsely *(page 7)*

imprinted *(im-PRINT-id)* marked in a way that cannot be removed *(page 6)*

invalid *(in-VAL-id)* no longer true or workable *(page 8)*

limitations *(lim-i-TAY-shuhnz)* restrictions *(page 5)*

safeguards *(SAYF-gahrdz)* security measures *(page 15)*

secure *(si-KYOOR)* safe *(page 8)*

transaction *(tran-ZAK-shuhn)* the act of giving things in order to receive other things *(page 8)*

vendors *(VEN-duhrz)* people who sell goods or services *(page 5)*

Index

Focus on
Social Studies

Purpose To explore how money was used in early societies

What to Do

The earliest metal coins were made in the seventh century B.C.E. in an area that is now Turkey. Since then, metal coins have been in constant use.

Step 1 ▸ Work with a partner. Choose an ancient civilization, such as Egypt, Rome, or China.

Step 2 ▸ Now research the civilization's earliest use of coins. When were they first used? What were the coins made of? Who used them, and what were they used for?

Step 3 ▸ Make a poster showing images of the coins and their values. Write several fact boxes explaining the origins and forms of the coins.

Step 4 ▸ Present your poster to the class.